The Ethics and Consequences of War

Table Of Contents

Prologue: War and Its Realities

In human history, war has cast its shadow, leaving a trail of devastation and suffering. In these dark moments, the true nature of conflict reveals itself, exposing the gruesome realities that have plagued our world since time immemorial. Within this context, I embark on this journey to write a book that explores the multifaceted aspects of war, drawing from my own experiences and the lessons that can be gleaned from them.

Let me take you back to 1999, a year etched in my memory for the haunting encounters I faced. In Monrovia, a city caught between two wars, a temporary peace allowed me to reunite with my father and little brother. The journey was difficult, as checkpoints operated by armed forces resembled scenes from a war movie. At each stop, my father had to offer money to ensure our safe passage.

The war's impact was starkly evident when I reached my brother's bedroom, where a massive hole bore witness to a recent shell explosion. He was only thirteen years old, yet already exposed to the horrors of war. My brother proposed an outing as evening fell, concealed from our father. We found ourselves in a bar, unknowingly sharing space with Chuckie, the son of Charles Taylor, a notorious figure known for his ruthless nature. My brother warned me not to stare, emphasizing the inherent danger around him.

Monrovia itself stood as a testament to war's destructive force. Bullet marks scarred the walls, remnants of a city ravaged by conflict. However, amidst the desolation, the landscape's natural beauty persisted, with spectacular beaches starkly contrasting the human-made devastation. During our two-week stay, we encountered harrowing stories that illuminated the true face of war. When the time came to depart, I couldn't help but feel a twinge of guilt, leaving my father and brother behind. However, I soon realized that they were where they needed to be, providing aid and support to those caught amid the chaos.

War had already touched my life before that experience. In 1991, the civil war in the Democratic Republic of Congo forced my mother, brother, and me to flee, leaving my father behind to tend to his business. In 1997, during a vacation in Kinshasa, a conflict between Rwanda and the Democratic Republic of Congo erupted, causing serious consequences for Rwandan citizens residing in the area. We were forced to abandon our home and seek refuge with an aunt. On that same day, a desperate Rwandan friend sought shelter on our aunt's terrace, concealed among stacked metal storage trunks. During the night, the police arrived, alerted by informants who claimed that Rwandans were hiding in the apartment. Our suitcases were ransacked, and my mother and aunt were taken into custody. We contacted my grandfather, a Congolese Colonel, who eventually secured their release after several arduous hours. Seeking safety, we took shelter in the Belgium Hotel, whose name bore similarity to the embassy, offering temporary sanctuary from the chaos. However, even there, we were not immune to the terror of war. A chance encounter with a soldier, weapon pointed at me, triggered intense fear as he demanded I join others already on the floor, arms raised. Only when we understood that they were searching for Rwandans suspected of hiding weapons did a collective sense of relief wash over us.

This book aims to provide insight into the complex nature of conflicts that have affected our world and their significant impact on humanity. These experiences are deeply etched into my being, forming the backdrop for exploring war's complexities and profound impact on individuals and societies. In the following pages, I will delve into the intricate tapestry of war, weaving together historical analysis, personal narratives, and thought-provoking insights.

My personal experiences with war have served as a profound education, revealing the depths of human suffering and resilience. The horrors unleashed during times of war spare no aspect of life, inflicting wounds that run deep and linger long after the guns have fallen silent. Witnessing the devastating impact of conflicts on individuals, families, and entire nations has left an indelible mark on my consciousness.

The lessons learned from personal experiences with war are both humbling and sobering. They teach us the futility and senselessness of violence, urging us to seek peaceful solutions to conflicts. They remind us of the importance of empathy and compassion, for it is through understanding the pain of others that we can forge paths to reconciliation and healing. War's relentless onslaught compels us to confront our prejudices and biases, challenging us to rise above the divisions that fuel conflict and strive for a more just and inclusive world.

Also, these experiences ignite a fierce determination to prevent future generations from enduring the horrors of war. They fuel a commitment to work tirelessly for peace, justice, and equality. Armed with the knowledge of war's devastating consequences, we are compelled to become agents of change, standing against the forces perpetuating violence and destruction.

Sharing these personal experiences through the written word is both cathartic and transformative. Through these stories, we can cultivate empathy, challenge apathy, and foster a global community that values diplomacy, understanding, and the inherent dignity of every human being. I hope that by opening a window into the realities of war, this book can inspire readers to reflect on the true cost of conflicts and kindle a collective desire for lasting peace.

In examining the historical context surrounding each conflict, we strive to unearth the root causes, the geopolitical complexities, and the societal factors that contribute to the outbreak and escalation of wars. By understanding the broader picture, you can begin comprehending the systemic issues and structural inequalities perpetuating violence cycles, enabling us to envision a more peaceful future.

I sincerely hope that this exploration of war's multifaceted realities will foster empathy, prompting readers to connect with the experiences of those directly affected by these conflicts. Through empathy, we can begin to grasp the true human cost of war, cultivating a deep understanding of the suffering endured by individuals and communities caught in its grasp.

In the end, this book is not just a collection of stories and analysis; it is an invitation to imagine a future where peace triumphs over the devastation of war. It is a call to action, urging us to advocate for diplomacy, reconciliation, and justice. By understanding war's complexities, we can collectively strive for a world where conflicts are resolved through dialogue, compassion replaces aggression, and wounds inflicted by war can heal. Let's take a look at what the content of this book entails.

In Chapter 1, "War and The World of God: What the Bible Says about War," I will explore the intersection of war and religion, delving into various religious perspectives on warfare and seeking wisdom from sacred texts to understand the ethical and moral dimensions of armed conflicts.

In Chapter 2, "Modern Wars and Causes," I will examine contemporary conflicts' underlying causes and catalysts. From political and economic factors to ideological and territorial disputes, I will unpack the complex web of reasons that fuel wars in our modern age, striving to uncover the patterns that persist across different geographical regions.

In Chapter 3, I will explore the Sierra Leone Civil War, a devastating conflict gripping the nation for over a decade. Through personal accounts, historical analysis, and expert interviews, I will strive to comprehend the complexities of this war and its lasting impact on the people and the country.

In Chapter 4, I will turn its focus to the wars that have plagued Liberia. I will delve into the last four wars that tore through the nation, examining the underlying causes, key players, and the repercussions that continue to shape Liberia's trajectory.

In Chapter 5, I will focus on the KIVU Conflict, an ongoing struggle that has ravaged the Democratic Republic of Congo. Through extensive research and first-hand testimonies, we will shed light on the intricate dynamics of this complex conflict, exploring its historical roots, regional implications, and the role of external actors.

Finally, Chapter 6 will be dedicated to examining the far-reaching impacts of wars on our world. From human suffering and displacement to economic devastation and environmental degradation, we will strive to comprehend the immense toll conflicts exact on individuals, communities, and the global stage.

As I have mentioned, my Personal experiences with war have served as a profound education, revealing the depths of human suffering and resilience. The horrors unleashed during times of war spare no aspect of life, inflicting wounds that run deep and linger long after the guns have fallen silent. Witnessing the devastating impact of conflicts on individuals, families, and entire nations has left an indelible mark on my consciousness.

As you navigate the pages of this book, I urge you to join me on a path toward empathy and understanding. Through the personal narratives shared, you will witness the raw emotions, the untold stories, and the human toll war inflicts upon individuals, families, and entire societies. These personal accounts serve as a poignant reminder that real lives are being shattered behind the statistics and headlines, and futures are being irreversibly altered.

By encouraging critical thinking and reflection, I hope to provoke a deeper examination of the justifications, motivations, and consequences of armed conflicts. Moreover, I aim to ignite introspection within you, challenging preconceived notions and questioning the narratives surrounding the war. This introspection will enable you to confront your biases and prejudices, allowing for a more nuanced and compassionate understanding of the complexities inherent in war.

Central to my mission is the desire to foster meaningful dialogue. By creating spaces for open and respectful conversations, we can collectively challenge the status quo, challenge the narratives perpetuating violence, and actively seek alternative paths toward conflict resolution. I urge you to engage in discussions, share your thoughts, and actively pursue peace.

So, come with me on this transformative journey. Together, let us navigate the complex realities of war, guided by empathy, introspection, and the unwavering belief that peace is attainable. By comprehensively understanding war, we take the first step towards shaping a future where the horrors of armed conflict are relegated to the annals of history and where the enduring human spirit triumphs over the shadows of violence.

Chapter 1: War and The Word of God

The Bible is full of accounts of wars. Some of these wars even documented biblical accuracy as archeology has unveiled artifacts with data confirming their records exactly as recorded in the Bible.

After the creation of non-living and living things, including man, God put a man in the Garden of Eden and pronounced that it was good until man fell through disobedience. Because God gave man free will, they could decide to do evil or obey God. We live in an ecosystem where evil and good men are at war.

God hates war; meanwhile, preserving order on earth and defeating those who want to abolish good things is essential. The first recorded war was in heaven, where Lucifer and his angels combat God and his angels. But God won the war through Christ Jesus.

One objection always raised against faith is the violence revealed in the Old Testament. Israel seemed violent, and God appeared like a domineering warmonger. Joshua, Gideon, and David were among those who overcame and killed the enemies in the name of the Lord. In this chapter, we shall examine what the Bible says about war.

The Underlying Message of War In The Scripture

There are more than four hundred references to war in the Bible. When these are broken down, you'll see that they include instances of interpersonal and military conflicts. The scripture says there's "a time to love, and a time to hate; a time for war, and a time for peace" (Ecclesiastes 3:8).

The old folks used to plan battles according to God's time and purpose. God described his people in Jeremiah 51:20 as "my hammer and weapon of war: with you, I break nations in pieces; with you I destroy kingdoms." Also, Jesus Christ predicted that his second coming would be preceded by wars and rumors of wars (Matthew 24:6).

Families, communities, and countries engage in conflicts and wars, which lead to a painful legacy. Billy Graham says, "The Holy Scripture encourages us to supplicate for peace and promote people who work for peace. But the scripture also tells us that we can't end conflicts and wars completely."

The next generations will go back to those conflicts in emotional or physical ways, hurling insults or bullets back and forth. Any peace between conventionally hostile neighbors or nations is suspicious. The two parties know that a new conflict may arise out of bitterness or defeat. The defeated party will nurture a quest for vengeance.

The arsenal of wars included guns, swords, and cannons. There's always a tendency for people or nations living together or side by side with unsettled tensions to pick up their arsenals for a fresh attack. There will always be War on earth till the second coming of Jesus Christ.

Old Testament Bloodshed

There are many examples of military engagement in the Old Testament where Israelites were defeated by oppressors or were instructed to kill their enemies. For insurance, a cursory reading of the book of Joshua can trigger questions that may leave us angry, confused, or give up on God. Why would God, who created heaven and earth and everything in it, order people to loot a land that belonged to another nation?

The book of Joshua in the Old Testament is particularly overwhelming, but Andy Patton argues that we must peruse it in its context. The Lord sent his chosen people, the Israelites, into lands he had set aside as their inheritance. Israelites defeated lands and killed people.   There is much violence on earth. Imagine an idolatrous nation indulging in pagan rituals, such as rejecting and mocking the only true God and child sacrifice.

Another story of war in the Bible that can baffle someone is when God ordered King Saul to go to the land of Amalek and destroy them. The war was initiated to take revenge on Amalekites opposing children of Israel while they were coming from Egypt. But as Any Patton has said that the scripture should be studied contextually. Most Old Testament books are full of war. Why would God decide to destroy an entire nation for another? Even the same God that ordered Israelites to destroy other nations also ordered other nations to destroy Israelites and even sent them into exile for disobeying him.

The Root of Judgment

Canaan did not come from another account of creation. The Canaanites were part of the descendants of Ham, the second son of Noah. People slain by Joshua and his army were made like God after his likeness and came from Adam and Eve.

However, what brought about judgement through war was that they allowed themselves to be misled to reject God and turned to debauched religious beliefs. They're guilty of disobedience against God's statutes, the roots implanted in them when God shapes them. It's an abomination for any God's creation to worship anyone except Him. God's statutes existed even before God gave Moses the ten commandments and exposed his chosen nation to the doctrine of religious leaders.

Apostle Paul explains in Romans 2:15, "The work of the law is written on their hearts, while their conscience also bears witness, and their conflicting thoughts accuse or even excuse them." The children of Canaan stood accused.

The Biblical Fiber Point Of The War

When Joshua led his men into war, they were not destroying a regular nation; that was a military outpost. As Joshua Ryan Butler explained, "God was destroying the Great Wall of China, not Beijing."

Also, Patton lets us know that God created limits and boundaries that limited Joshua's military prosecution. Some parts of Canaan land were ordered to be left out, and Israelites were ordered to have mercy upon them and even invite them to worship God, which few Canaanites accepted, and many refused to worship God.

Though some said it was a mercy that inspired the Israelites to spare lives where God said destroyed all, the Israelites understood that God had a purpose for every instruction he dishes out.

God isn't gratuitous, nor does he delight in killing or destroying. The Almighty God hates hands that shed innocent blood, hearts that plan evil plans, and feet that easily run to evil (Proverbs 6:17-18).

Andy Patton explains that the language of warfare may be full of rhetoric and hyperbole, extreme war language generally among the writings of old nations. Vividly, when a town is said to be destroyed, this cannot be all cases if remnants of that nation are explaining the events they witnessed.

Though war is always full of bloodshed, it has a divine purpose. God's purpose for all wars is for evils to be wiped out, and God should be known as Sovereign God. God never enjoys violence.

New Testament Wars

During the time of Jesus Christ, Israel was a defeated nation because they perpetually decided to worship idols instead of God. Even when God had caused division among the twelve tribes due to their disobedience. They had been divided into two kingdoms- the Southern Kingdom and the Northern Kingdom. God also sent them into exile. Part of them came back to their land, but some never received the grace to return. Rome colonized them when Jesus Christ was born, crucified, died, buried, resurrected, and ascended to heaven.

God displayed his all-sufficient power with the few men who defeated the Midianites. The issue was internal. The eponymous epistle writer of James 4:1 asks, "What springs up fights and quarrels among you?" War doesn't halt because there's an internal and unpleasant battle within the Christians, the war to defeat sin. That's the only form of war that transpired in the New Testament.

Christ didn't come on Earth to deal with physical battles because the Earth is spiritual, and He understood that the real problem on Earth is internal strife. Little wonder James 4:1 says, "Your passions are at war within you."

When Christ cured the paralytic, he said, "Take heart, my son, your sins are forgiven" (Matthew 9:2). The most significant enemy is preventing people from encountering eternal life with Christ

Jesus rather than influencing them to experience eternal damnation with the devil.

The most ruthless enemy of individuals is SATAN. That's why believers are inspired to love their enemies and wear the armor of God against Satan and sin. When dealing with sin or Satan, your real weapon must be the Word of God.

Apostle Paul taught the believers at Corinth to combat sin with the tools of our warfare, which are not of the flesh but have divine power to destroy strongholds (2 Corinthians 10:4).

The Coming End Times of War

Believers await a final, huge confrontation between Jesus Christ and Satan. Christ Jesus has come to deliver his people from sin, and Satan wasn't pleased with that, for he wanted everyone to be his own, which is contrary to the Will of God for humanity. Also, this world will pass away, and the new earth and new heaven will emerge where Jesus Christ will reign for a certain number of years. Satan is striving with believers to abort this plan.

The war that would occur between Christ and Satan would be so dramatic. However, the winner is known already, which is Christ Jesus. But the details are not clear in the Bible. Historical wars are explained using language, but language cannot avail us to depict the final epic war. Revelation only gives clues, and most of the languages are symbolic.

Compared to the armies of Israel, Jesus Christ will follow through and entirely demolish Satan and his forces. Even Satan himself knows that victory is certain for Christ Jesus.

God authorized government authorities to enforce laws.

The USA has deliberately taken some measures to wipe out terrorists worldwide. After the invasion of terrorists on September 2001, the United States of America's government started to make some changes in national affairs to hedge against the future terrorist attack. There has been an increase in security operations in all countries. One of the American presidents pronounced war against terrorism. He launched a global coalition, and other nations are joining the train.

Everyone is experiencing changes in their lives. Nations are standing against nations, and the world is facing battle or under the threat of battle with portentous tools looming over the people. The evil of war is making the headlines daily with reports of attacks from biological, chemical, and nuclear weapons and conventional armament. The Bible doesn't keep us ignorant on this issue as it informs us it will perpetuate more and more as the second coming of Jesus Christ approaches.

According to Matthew 24:6-8, "And ye shall hear of wars and rumors of wars: see that ye be not troubled: for all these things must come to pass, but the end is not yet. For nation shall rise against nation, and kingdom against kingdom: and there shall be famines, pestilences, and earthquakes, in diverse places. All these are the beginning of sorrows."

The millennial reign of Jesus will be void of terrors and wars.

A war that brings killing, violence, and other destruction will only cease if the kingdom of God comes on earth today. The sign that the kingdom of God has come on earth is when all the inhabitants have received Christ Jesus as their personal Lord and Savior, and they're all yielding to God. The second coming of Jesus Christ is fast approaching. During His millennial reign, Christ will rule with an iron rod, and Satan, with his followers, will be chained and destroyed. During the millennial reign, there won't be a war for Satan, who has been influencing men to do evil.

When we enter the millennial reign of Jesus Christ, the earth shall be void of tribulation and experience rest. Christ is the only solution to end the war on Earth. Enmity keeps on in the heart of men because there's no love. Where love doesn't exist, a hatred that produces enmity reigns. Satan stirs up the hearts of men, which causes them to wage war against their fellow humans. Until the hearts of men become the kingdom of our Lord and His Christ, war will continue to transpire in the world.

Key Takeaways

- Though part of the Bible is full of war, God doesn't delight in violence. He wants the whole world to know Him and serve Him alone.

- It's an abomination for God's creation to worship other gods. We're created for God alone, and we must worship him alone. Any nation that refuses to worship God would experience a war that will put them to ruin.

- God's intention for every nation that faces war is to wipe out the evil-doing in the nation, and good deeds should reign in such a nation.

- The world is spiritual. Every war is not physical; it's spiritual. Satan stirs the hearts of men to wage war against one another. War won't cease to happen on earth unless men's hearts are full of God's love.

- During the millennial reign of Christ Jesus, Satan would have been chained and his followers destroyed. The earth will rest because the Prince of Peace, Jesus Christ, will reign on earth then.

Chapter 2: The Modern Wars and Causes

Even if you have not heard about the no-ending Israel vs. Palestine war or America vs. Iran, the recent one that broke out between Russia and Ukraine is one everyone can relate with. The fight looks like it is not ending soon, even though both countries have felt the negative impacts of the loss of peace ever since February 2022.

The word war is a common parlance among many people and peace-keeping experts. Even people who know little or nothing about wars have one or two things to say about it, especially those who lost their loved ones or partake in one or two. Wars create lasting, mostly negative effects, especially on the loser. The winner might draw solace and manage their loss from the fact that they won. But for the loser, it is a different ball game. They may have to forcefully adjust to their new reality because they have no option.

What Is War?

The word war has no universal definition. But we say that it is a state of armed conflicts between groups within a country or between different countries. We can also say it is a hostile competition between two groups or people. And lastly, we can say that it is a campaign against an undesirable activity or circumstance.

When we take a peep into the history of humanity, one thing we will likely find there is war. Wars have been a part of human history for many years. We can hardly read the history of a country or state, or local town without some elements related to the war in the background. In fact, war was what they were known for some countries. They conquered and took over many territories with wars.

However, in this modern day, war has been weaponized more than it has ever been. It is now a weapon in the hands of countries and people to threaten others. No thanks to technological and scientific advancement in this aspect. As technology advances, wars are becoming easier to fight. In fact, today, countries are investing heavily in procuring and purchasing weapons just because war might break out at any time. Powerful nations make many weapons of mass destruction to threaten and dominate others.

One common thing we have seen that has played out in many instances is that most leaders don't consider their citizens or soldiers' strength when they declare war, especially as it is played out today. They declare war as long as their interest is protected and their regime's control is preserved. This is the reason why many countries lose their citizens in a war they should not have started.

What is modern war?

Now that we have established what war is all about, we must dive into what modern war is and what the first modern war fought in human history is.

Modern wars are warfare fought with modern technology. These types of war are quite different from what was obtained in old times in terms of the methods, military concepts, strategies, and weaponry that are involved. When we say wars have been modernized, we mean a new system of fighting wars has emerged, which has a notable contrast with the previous systems and strategies.

One thing about modern war is that it emphasizes how combatants must modernize to preserve their battle worthiness and strength. And as such, it is an evolving concept, regarded differently in terms of places and times.

However, in its broad sense, modern wars include the use of the 'gunpowder revolution' that marks the start of early modern warfare, but other landmark military developments have been used instead. The first modern war was fought is the American Civil War in the modern age. Two sides involved advances in military technology and communications to revolutionize the way wars are fought. The American Civil War was regarded as the first modern war. It was the first war where the widespread use of electrified and mechanized weapons like rifles, telegraphs, aerial observation, railroad trains, torpedoes, photography, mines, and ironclad ships occurred. Although most of these devices were used for military purposes during the wars, the soldiers sometimes refused to use new technologies. On occasion, the entrepreneurs and investors of these new devices visualized military devices for them and had to persuade the soldiers to use them in the military efforts. The soldiers of the nineteenth century were not trained with those sophisticated weapons, so using the new gadgets posed many problems for them.

Causes Of Modern Wars

It is rare to find a single reason why wars happen. The causes of wars, especially ones that we can relate to today, are linked with many reasons which can be somehow intertwined in the most complicated ways.

Many experts and theories have been put forth to discuss possible reasons why most modern wars happen.

Economic Gain

Most times, war breaks out between two countries because one country wishes to take control or influence another country's economic value. Even when they don't openly declare it, the underlying factor or reason for conflict is tied to it, even if there may be other reasons why war can occur; economic motive is the underlying reason for most modern conflict.

In time past, the gains of a warring country might be something like silver or gold. It may even be livestock, such as horses and cattle. But in recent times, it is known as imperialism - a system where a nation is seeking to take or control the natural resources of another. Even though every nation knows its boundaries and can identify what belongs to them, some countries might want to have undue influence over others because of their economic value. Historical examples of wars fought for economic gain are the Anglo-Indian Wars between 1766-1849, the Opium Wars of 1839-1860, and the Japanese Invasion of Manchuria 1931-1932.

Territorial Gain

A nation might decide it needs more living space for agricultural use or other purposes. Territory can also be used as "buffer zones" between two hostile enemies. Buffer zones are proxy conflicts that are fought indirectly between opposing powers in a third country. Each power will support the side which best suits military, logistical, and economic interests. The buffer zones known as proxy wars are common during the Cold War.

Unaccountability

If we consider Russia's invasion of Ukraine, we will understand better why war broke out. When a personalized autocrat like Putin is running a country, the possibility of going to war, even when it is unnecessary, is imminent. Most leaders don't weigh the interest of their people and military strength before they declare war. Like Putin, they can pursue whatever helps them preserve their regime's control without recourse to how many souls will be lost and who will be affected by their actions. When leaders go unchecked and are not accountable to their people, they usually ignore the cost of fighting a war. They don't care about what happens to their people and what they might lose fighting wars. Instead, they pursue whatever aligns with their interest and are willing to get it at all costs, even if it would resort to war. The unaccountability of a leader is a recipe for war, especially senseless ones.

Lack of proper considerations / Uncertainty

Most leaders often don't consider other parties' strengths and capacities before declaring war. They only consider what they have and make hasty decisions. Most leaders don't know their enemy's resolve or strength. How strong is their military base? Which countries are they in alignment with that might come to their aid during the war? How capable are they of resisting? All these things are fundamentally uncertain issues that most had not considered before they ventured into them. Russia didn't know how unified the West would be against them when they invaded Ukraine. Putin thought it was going to be an easy ride. But surprisingly, they got a bad draw in all these areas.

There are ways a country can get reliable information about the country they are trying to invade. However, being uncertain doesn't mean the costs of war are uncertain, or an invasion is a gamble. You can't trust your enemy's demonstrations of resolve because there are numerous reasons to bluff, hoping to gain advantages without fighting. However, a lack of proper consideration and dialogue is the reason why many wars happen even when they could be avoided.

Differences in Ideological or philosophical stand

Let's consider Putin again. If you consider the reason why most recent wars happen, you will notice that it is mostly about Putin's nationalist obsessions and desires for an inglorious legacy. Before the war broke out, Putin was willing to pay anything in pursuit of his ideology and glory. This is one of the unreasonable reasons why wars happen. Most leaders have intangible and ideological incentives for war, which drives them above their people's interest.

Moving from the leaders, we can say that societies have ideological incentives too. Unlike the people of Belarus, the Ukrainians refused to accept serious restrictions on their sovereignty despite being presumed to have a weak military base, like the American revolutionaries who undertook the risks and ruins of fighting partly in pursuit of an ideal.

Bias

This is another cause of the modern war that can even be traced to the current one between Russia and Ukraine. Putin's isolation and isolation from the basic truth is why his egoistic behavior is common among leaders who think they have it all. And to worsen the case, his advisors grossly undermined the effect and the difficulty of war. This is what we can call institutional bias. In this system, the followers are unwilling to tell their leaders the dangers ahead but will be willing to follow their instructions without any form of advice. Autocrats are always prone to this problem. They always feel like they have everything it takes to initiate a war, even when they don't. That is also the case with some leaders of democracies too, but their case is associated with intelligence failures. Human beings are prone to bias somehow. In fact, we have the ability to cling to mistaken beliefs. Sometimes, we can be too overconfident in our capacity and underestimate others. It is the reason why we fight people even when we can settle things amicably. We are easily puffed up when we see that we have chances of victory. We demonize ourselves and misjudge our opponent's strengths. These misperceptions often bring many countries into war when they don't prepare for it.

In conclusion, modern wars are contemporary warfare that any of the issues discussed above can cause. However, wars could break out in relation to religious interference, imposition, or differences, especially among a set of people. That can also happen when it has to do with an ethnic group trying to usurp authority or claiming 'lord' over another. But when it comes to modern war, the issues discussed above might likely be why wars break out. And all these factors must be considered for a nation to avert possible war.

Key Takeaways

- Modern warfare is contemporary warfare; whereby technologically advanced technological weapons are used to fight wars.
- The first modern war was fought in the American Civil War in the modern age. One in which the two sides involved advances in military technology and communications to revolutionize the way wars are fought.
- Lack of accountability in leadership is a recipe for war, especially senseless ones.

Chapter 3: The Sierra Leone Civil War

The Sierra Leone Civil War was a tragic period in the history of West Africa. From 1991 to 2002, a brutal conflict caused immense suffering and devastation for the country's people. This chapter will delve into the causes, events, and aftermath of the Sierra Leone Civil War, aiming to shed light on the complexities of the conflict and its long-lasting impact.

In this chapter, I will explore the historical, political, and socioeconomic factors that contributed to the outbreak of the war. I will examine the grievances of the Sierra Leoneans, the rise of rebel groups, and the subsequent escalation of violence. Furthermore, I will analyze the role of external influences and the impact of regional and international intervention.

The chapter will also delve into the key actors involved in the conflict, including government forces, rebel groups, and the various regional and international entities that played a role in shaping the trajectory of the war. During this period, I will investigate the atrocities that involved the enlistment of child soldiers and the utilization of sexual violence as a tool of warfare. Additionally, I will analyze the humanitarian crisis that arose due to these actions.

I will explore the efforts to resolve the conflict and bring peace, including ceasefire agreements and peace negotiations. We will also examine the establishment of the Truth and Reconciliation Commission and the challenges faced in reconciliation and justice.

Finally, I will reflect on the long-term consequences of the Sierra Leone Civil War and its impact on the country's social, political, and economic landscape. From rebuilding efforts to the pursuit of justice and national healing, we will explore the steps taken to recover from the scars of the conflict and pave the way for a more stable and prosperous Sierra Leone.

By examining the Sierra Leone Civil War in detail, you aim to gain a comprehensive understanding of the causes, dynamics, and consequences of this tragic conflict, thereby illuminating the complexities of post-colonial societies and the challenges they face in their pursuit of peace, justice, and development.

How it Started

The Sierra Leone Civil War occurred from 1991 to 2002, causing great suffering to the people of the West African nation. The war was characterized by widespread violence, human rights abuses, and the use of child soldiers, leaving a deep and lasting impact on Sierra Leonean society. It was a devastating conflict that engulfed the country.

A complex web of socioeconomic, political, and regional factors primarily fueled the civil war. Despite its abundant natural resources like diamonds, Sierra Leone faces challenges of extreme poverty, economic inequality, and limited opportunities for its people. Corruption and mismanagement of resources further exacerbated these issues, leading to widespread discontent among the population.

Political factors also influenced the outbreak of the war in Sierra Leone. After gaining independence, the country went through a period of political instability, with coups and military interventions adding to the turmoil. The authoritarian rule, lack of democracy, and ethnic tensions created a volatile environment, fostering grievances that would eventually manifest as armed rebellion.

The Revolutionary United Front (RUF), led by Foday Sankoh, and the National Patriotic Front of Liberia (NPFL), led by Charles Taylor, were the primary rebel groups involved in the conflict. These groups sought to overthrow the government and gain control over Sierra Leone's rich diamond mines and other valuable resources. Their tactics included brutal attacks on civilians, mass killings, sexual violence, and the systematic recruitment of child soldiers.

The war witnessed the involvement of regional and international actors. To restore peace and stability, the Economic Community of West African States (ECOWAS) created the Economic Community of West African States Monitoring Group (ECOMOG) and intervened. The United Nations also played a crucial role by establishing the United Nations Mission in Sierra Leone (UNAMSIL) to support the peace process.

The Sierra Leone Civil War resulted in a severe humanitarian crisis, with thousands of people displaced and widespread atrocities committed against civilians. Local and international organizations undertook efforts to provide humanitarian aid and address the urgent needs of the affected population.

Ceasefire agreements, peace negotiations, and international interventions eventually ended the conflict. The Lomé Peace Agreement in 1999 and the Comprehensive Peace Agreement in 2002 marked significant milestones towards achieving lasting peace. Furthermore, the establishment of the Truth and Reconciliation Commission aimed to address past grievances, promote healing, and facilitate national reconciliation.

The war's aftermath posed significant challenges for Sierra Leone, including post-war reconstruction, disarmament, demobilization, and reintegration of former combatants, and the pursuit of justice for war crimes. The country embarked on a path of recovery, focusing on rebuilding infrastructure, strengthening democratic institutions, and promoting economic development.

The Sierra Leone Civil War is a stark reminder of the devastating consequences of internal conflicts and the immense challenges faced in post-war transitions. Understanding this war's causes, events, and aftermath is essential in comprehending Sierra Leone's history and drawing lessons that can contribute to peacebuilding efforts in similar contexts globally.

Socioeconomic Factors

- Unequal distribution of wealth and resources: Sierra Leone's natural resources, such as diamonds, were controlled by a small elite, leading to stark economic disparities.

- High levels of poverty and unemployment, especially among youth: Most of the population faced extreme poverty and limited employment opportunities, exacerbating social tensions.

- Limited access to basic services: Education and healthcare were inadequately provided, particularly in rural areas, further exacerbating socioeconomic inequalities.

Corruption and Mismanagement of Resources:

- Rampant corruption at various levels of government: Widespread corruption undermined the efficient allocation of resources and eroded public trust in institutions.

- The exploitation of natural resources, particularly diamonds, by a few elite groups: The illicit diamond trade fueled conflict and enriched a select few while most of the population remained impoverished.

- Lack of accountability in revenue management and resource allocation: Mismanagement of resources and lack of transparency contributed to the economic grievances of the population.

Lack of Economic Opportunities:

- Limited employment opportunities and income generation: The absence of diversified industries and sustainable economic programs resulted in widespread unemployment and underemployment.

- Absence of sustainable development programs and inclusive economic policies: The government's failure to implement effective development strategies hindered economic growth and perpetuated inequality.

- Discontent among marginalized groups and rural communities: Economic marginalization of rural areas and ethnic minorities deepened grievances, creating a fertile ground for rebel recruitment.

Political Factors

- Decades of political instability and military interventions: Sierra Leone experienced a series of coups, including the 1967 and 1992 military takeovers, undermining democratic governance.

- Suppression of political dissent and restriction of civil liberties: Political opposition and civil society groups faced repression, stifling political participation and exacerbating grievances.

- Limited democratic institutions and lack of participatory governance: Weak institutions and a lack of transparency and accountability in governance further alienated the population.

Ethnic Tensions and Regional Divides:

- Historical, ethnic divisions and inequalities: Long-standing ethnic divisions, particularly between the Mende and Temne ethnic groups, were exploited for political gain, leading to tensions.

- Unequal distribution of political power and resources along regional lines: Disparities in resource allocation and political representation between the north and south fueled regional grievances and conflicts.

- Identity politics and manipulation of ethnic affiliations: Political leaders manipulated ethnic identities to mobilize support and consolidate power, further deepening divisions.

Discontent with the Government and its Policies:

- Popular dissatisfaction with governance and public services: Widespread dissatisfaction with the government's performance, including failing to address economic and social issues, eroded public trust.

- Perceived marginalization and exclusion of certain groups: Certain communities and regions felt marginalized and excluded from decision-making processes, exacerbating social tensions.

- Lack of political representation and accountability: Citizens' voices were not adequately represented, and the absence of mechanisms for holding government officials accountable deepened public discontent.

Support for Rebel Groups:

- Regional support: The National Patriotic Front of Liberia (NPFL), led by Charles Taylor, provided training, arms, and logistical support to the Revolutionary United Front (RUF) rebels.

- The exploitation of Sierra Leone's resources: External actors were involved in the illicit diamond trade, supporting rebel groups in exchange for access to valuable resources.

- Proxy wars and regional instability: The Sierra Leone conflict became intertwined with the regional conflicts in Liberia and the broader dynamics of West Africa.

Arms Trafficking and Mercenary Activities:

- The proliferation of small arms: Illicit arms trade flooded Sierra Leone with weapons, escalating the intensity and brutality of the conflict.

- The influx of foreign mercenaries: Foreign mercenaries were recruited by rebel groups, further fueling the violence and contributing to the breakdown of security.

Failure of International Intervention:

- Limited international response and attention: The international community initially paid limited attention to the conflict, delaying effective intervention.

- Challenges in peacekeeping and humanitarian efforts: Peacekeeping missions faced logistical challenges, and the humanitarian response struggled to address the magnitude of the crisis.

- Slow response to root causes: The focus on short-term stabilization overshadowed efforts to address the underlying socioeconomic and political factors driving the conflict.

Key Actors in the Conflict

The Sierra Leone Civil War involved various key actors who played significant roles in shaping the course and dynamics of the conflict. These actors included government forces, rebel groups, regional entities, and international actors. Here is an overview of the key actors involved:

- Revolutionary United Front (RUF)

Foday Sankoh led the RUF as the primary rebel group involved in the conflict.

The RUF employed brutal tactics, including recruiting child soldiers and using violence against civilians. The group sought to overthrow the government and gain control over Sierra Leone's valuable diamond mines.

- Armed Forces Revolutionary Council (AFRC):

The AFRC was a group of military officers who seized power in a coup in 1997, aligning themselves with the RUF.

They formed a short-lived military junta that further destabilized the country.

- Government Forces:

The government of Sierra Leone, represented by the Sierra Leone Army, fought against the rebel groups.

However, the government forces faced challenges, including corruption, poor discipline, and inadequate resources.

- National Patriotic Front of Liberia (NPFL):

Led by Charles Taylor, the NPFL played a significant role in the Sierra Leone Civil War.

Taylor supported the RUF, including training, weapons, and logistical assistance.

His involvement was driven by regional power dynamics and his interest in Sierra Leone's resources.

- Economic Community of West African States Monitoring Group (ECOMOG):

ECOMOG was a regional military intervention force established by the Economic Community of West African States (ECOWAS).

ECOMOG deployed troops to Sierra Leone to support the government and restore peace and stability.

- United Nations Mission in Sierra Leone (UNAMSIL):

UNAMSIL was a United Nations peacekeeping mission deployed in Sierra Leone.

It was crucial in facilitating peace, disarming combatants, and restoring stability.

- Civil Society and Humanitarian Organizations:

Local civil society organizations, human rights groups, and humanitarian organizations assisted affected communities and advocated for peace and justice.

They played a vital role in documenting human rights abuses and supporting the process of national healing and reconciliation.

In conclusion, the Sierra Leone Civil War was devastating from a complex web of socioeconomic, political, and external factors. The war was fueled by deep-seated grievances arising from economic disparities, corruption, and lack of opportunities. Political instability, regional influences, and the exploitation of resources exacerbated tensions and provided fertile ground for rebellion. The conflict resulted in widespread human rights abuses, displacement, and loss of life. It took the efforts of regional and international actors to bring about a resolution and restore stability to Sierra Leone.

Key Takeaways

- Socioeconomic factors, such as poverty, unequal distribution of resources, and corruption, contributed to the grievances that fueled the conflict.

- Political factors, including authoritarian rule, regional tensions, and lack of democratic governance, further exacerbated the underlying tensions and divisions within the country.

- The involvement of external actors, particularly the support provided by Charles Taylor's NPFL and the exploitation of resources, added complexity to the conflict and prolonged its duration.

Chapter 4: The Liberian War

When we dive into African countries to count one or two countries that were bedeviled by wars, we would barely mention a few before we got to Liberia. Between 1989 and 2003, the country's and its citizens' existence were threatened by two different internal wars. The first Liberian War was one of Africa's bloodiest, with over 200,000 lives lost, many properties destroyed, and millions of Liberians scattered across neighboring countries. The Second Civil War ravaged the country and almost tore it into pieces as well. Over 50,000 souls were lost, and many properties were destroyed.

Let's dive into each of these wars and examine their effect on the country and its people.

The First Liberian Civil War

Undoubtedly, the First Liberian Civil War, which happened between 1989 and 1997, is Africa's bloodiest war. Not only that many lives and properties were lost, but the entire nation's economic and social systems also crumbled. Being the first country in West Africa to face a series of two civil wars within a few years, the country's democratic system and political structure were truncated, and this had a significant ripple effect on both the country and its people.

How the war broke out

On December 24, 1989, a rebel band known as the National Patriotic Front of Liberia led by Charles Taylor invaded Liberia from the Ivory Coast. This rebel group consisted mostly of Mano and Gio peoples from Nimba County in eastern Liberia. These sets of tribes have long stood against the rulership of Samuel Doe and his ethnic group known as Krahn. Among the people who were included in Taylor's NPFL were Liberian military men and civilians. In fact, this group was the first to recruit men as soldiers forcefully, and they clashed with government forces and other ethnic militias backing President Doe between December 1989 to mid-1993. During that time, all groups engaged in the war led to many civilian casualties because they were not well-trained for war. But when you consider how many lives were lost and what was responsible for the casualties, you will understand that they were Taylor's fault. In fact, his group were responsible for slaughtering thousands of Liberians, both civilians and soldiers, who stood against him. He killed both old and young people who were strongly against him and targeted mainly the Khran people from among President Doe Samuel. As the NPFL forces moved toward Monrovia, the country's capital city, in 1990, they started to go after people of Krahn extractions to weaken the President's homestead. They felt like killing their relatives would score many points in the war. They also didn't spare the Mandingo people, who were loyal to the Doe government to the core.

However, when it looks like more civilians are dying, and the government is losing more than necessary in terms of its citizens. The ECOWAS troop of the Nigerian and Ghanaian Army entered Monrovia for peacekeeping, but their presence lengthened the way by adding more strength to the President's hard-pressed troops. The most unfortunate event was that President Doe was captured and killed on September 9, 1990, by Prince Johnson and his rebel group, the Independent National Patriotic Front of Liberia

(INPFL), which had been orchestrating a campaign of calumny against the government. However, after Doe was captured, Taylor made its way to Monrovia to capture it, but the ECOWAS prevented him. That led to the formation of an Interim Government of National Unity (IGNU) led by Dr Amos C Sawyer, who later became the nation's President. However, Taylor refused to work with the interim arrangement and continued fighting. As the fight continued, many factions joined the conflict, including the Lofa National Patriotic Front of Liberia, the Armed Forces of Liberia, the Lofa Defense Force, and other security organizations that pledged their allegiance to the Doe's government. But unfortunately, the war ended on a tragic note as Doe lost the seat of power. Charles Taylor became the nation's President after his war strategies and influence gained momentum, and he overpowered the government.

The Second Liberian War

After Charles Taylor's first civil war victory, the country experienced peace and tranquility for two years. But shortly after the second year, another invasion occurred. This happened when an anti-Taylor rebel group supported by the government of Guinea and the Liberian United for Reconciliation and Democracy invaded the northern part of the country in 1999. These groups started gaining ground and winning the war against Taylor in the Northern part and headed to the state capital, Monrovia, by early 2002. In early 2003, another anti-Taylor group known as the Movement for Democracy in Liberia started attacking Taylor's government and eventually conquered the whole Southern, leaving the government with only two-thirds of the entire nation. Before the end of that year, the nation became ungovernable for him as the Siege of Monrovia mounted pressure on Taylor to vacate the seat for proper democratic government. When the pressure was much on him, Taylor resigned and fled to Nigeria. The warring parties signed the Accra Comprehensive Peace Agreement a week after, marking the end of political struggle and announcing the country's transition to democracy. One thing we must not forget anytime we discuss this Second Civil War is the wanton destruction and the loss of lives that greeted the unfortunate event. It is sad to note that over 50,000 people lost their lives while thousands were internally displaced. An interim arrangement was instituted by the National Transitional Government led by President Gyude Bryant. President Bryant governed the nation after the country's 2005 general elections.

My Liberian War experience

The Liberian Wars are not what I read on the pages of a book; I have many things I can tell as someone who experienced the war in person. I hope reading this will help you understand what transpired during these wars.

In 1999, everything seemed peaceful in Monrovia, the country's state capital, so I decided to see my father and my little brother. I argued a lot with my father, and after several negotiations, he accepted and sent us the money to buy the ticket. I took my little sister with me. When we arrived at the airport, the customs officer took my passport and kept it. She wanted money! I saw my father after the gate and explained with my hands, and he quickly understood and gave them money.

There were a lot of checkpoints with militaries on the way, like a war movie. At each checkpoint, my father had to give money.

In my brother's bedroom there is a huge hole. He was telling me that a shell hit a few weeks ago. He was 13 years old. After dinner, he proposes to go out without telling our father. It seemed that it was his habit, so we went to a bar, and the son of Charles Taylor, Chuckie, was there. I didn't know him; my little brother told me who he was and to not look for long at him because he was very dangerous and could kill someone for nothing. So we stayed a little and went back home.

Monrovia, the city, was totally destroyed by the war; all the infrastructure was with bullet marks on the walls. But the landscape was fabulous, and the beaches were spectacular. We stayed for two weeks, seeing and hearing very hard stories. When we left my father and my brother, I felt guilty, but both of them were helping a lot of people at that time, and it seemed that they were where they were supposed to be at that time.

In conclusion, wars have never left a country better than it was. They would rather tear a nation apart or slow the pace at which a nation is developing.

Most times, what's lost during wars is irreversible. Today, many people have lost their lives, and many properties are destroyed because of senseless wars that could have been avoided. That's why we must all choose the path of peace. That is non-negotiable and inevitable for any country to thrive in all ramifications. Peace is a life path we must all embrace as individuals and as nations.

Key Takeaways

- Liberia is the first West African country to experience a series of civil wars.
- Africa's bloodiest war was the First Liberian Civil War; over 200,000 souls were lost.
- Charles Taylor is the ringleader and sponsor of the first civil war that ousted President Samuel Doe as the country's leader
- He became the nation's President after his victory but was overthrown years after.

Chapter 5: The KIVU Conflicts

The Kivu conflict is a series of prolonged armed wars in the South Kivu and North Kivu in the Eastern Democratic Republic of Congo. The war has been transpiring since the end of Congo War II. Over one hundred and twenty armed groups, including the neighboring Ituri district, are potent in the Eastern DRC. Today, some active combatant groups are the Cooperative for the Development of Congo, the Allied Democratic Forces, some local Mai militias, and the 23 March Movement. Additionally, the United Nations force (MONUSCO) and East African Community regional force have intervened in the conflict.

The Kivu conflict started in 2004 in the Eastern Congo between the Hutu power group Democratic Groups for the Liberation of Rwanda (FDLR) and the armed Democratic Republic of Congo (FARDC). It consists of 3 phases; the third phase is a progressive conflict. Before March 2009, the major armed force opposing the FARDC was the

National Congress for the Defense of the People (CNDP). Following the discontinuance of conflict between these two hostile forces, combat Tutsi forces, formerly under the command of Laurent Nkunda, became the authoritative enemy of the government forces.

The Kivu conflict has the biggest peacekeeping mission, with a twenty-one thousand strong force. Meanwhile, on December 2017, 93 died in the region, with fifteen dying in a massive attack by an Islamist militia, the Allied Democratic Forces, in North Kivu. The peacekeeping force tends to circumvent the increased force in the conflict and reduce human rights abuses such as underage soldiers and sexual assault. MONUSCO has played a major role in the role. Hence, in this chapter, I will explore everything you need to know about the Kivu conflict, the key players, and the causes of the Kivu conflict.

The Key Players of The Kivu Conflict

Here are a few key players in the Kivu conflict:

The Congolese Armed Forces (FARDC)

FARDC was established in 2003 with 120,000 strong armies. Many were from the former combatant groups integrated following different peace deals. More than half of the Congolese soldiers were deployed in Eastern Congo. Since 2006, the Congolese government has tried twice to incorporate the six thousand rebel CNDP, but all effort was futile. In early 2009 the third attempt was made to integrate the CNDP and other remnants of rebel groups. The process was called fast-track accelerated incorporation. However, those who accepted to incorporate remained faithful to their former commanders, doubting the sustainability of the process.

National Congress for the Defense of the People (CNDP)

In July 2006, CNDP was launched. It's a Rwandan-backed rebel group created by Laurent Nkunda, a renegade Tutsi general. It aims to safeguard, defend and ensure political representation for many Congolese Tutsi dwelling in Eastern Congo and many Congolese refugees who are Tutsi dwelling in Rwanda. They have over six thousand combatants, including important members hired in Rwanda; many of its soldiers are Tutsi. Nkunda was banished on 5 January 2009 as a leader by Bosco Ntaganda, the military chief of staff. Subsequently, the CNDP became a political party.

Democratic Forces for the Liberation of Rwanda (FDLR)

FDLR is a Hutu militia group living in Eastern Congo. It devises to dethrone the Rwandan government and foster greater Hutu political representation. In 1994 in Rwanda, some of the leaders of FDLR indulged in genocide. In 2008 FDLR had 6,000 rebels, managing large provinces of the south and north Kivu, including the many major mining locations. Ignace Murwanashyaka is the president and supreme head of the FLDR, living in Germany. In November 2009, he was arrested for crimes against humanity and war crimes. Before 2009, the Congolese government had supported the group, but when its policy changed, it established military operations against FDLR.

Rally for Unity and Democracy (RUD)-Urunana

Since 2009, the RUD and the FDLR groups have reunited militarily. It is a splinter group of the FDLR. It has more than four hundred combatants living in North Kivu, with some dissident FDLR rebels. Jean-Marie Vianney Higiro, the first vice president of FDLR, created the group. He dwells in the United States, and other political leaders are in North America and Europe.

The causes of the crisis in North Kivu

The armed conflict burst forth in the North Kivu area in August 2007. Under the command of Laurent Nkunda, the renewed combat, the worst ever, the official DRC conflict pitted the CNDP armed political group against the regular

Congolese army. Mayi-mayi ethnic militia, CNDP, and the Rwandan FDLR were also involved. The Rwandan Hutu armed group, which consists of the remaining forces legally responsible for the 1994 Rwandan genocide, was also involved. UN peacekeeping forces in the MONUSCO and DRC couldn't withstand the war, so they only had to safeguard the population centers.

The major cause of the August combat was an attempt to incorporate CNDP allied forces into the FARDC. The renegade officer, Laurent Nkunda, claimed that CNDP forces were combating to safeguard the Tutsi population living in Eastern DRC from attack by the FDLR, which the CNDP allegedly accused the FARDC and Congolese government of supporting the group militarily. Also, mayi-mayi militias rage war against the CNDP. The mayi-mayi was created from an ethnic group intending to safeguard their ethnic group from enemies, CNDP, which accused the Rwandan government of supporting the group. Mayi-mayi militias were grouped in a political coalition known as PARECO.

Before December 2007, over five hundred thousand people ran away from their homes and secured shelter in camps or with host families. This prompted a severe humanitarian war. The civilians endured the consequences of the violence, which led to violations of humanitarian law and international human rights by the government's armed forces and the two-armed groups.

The increased war in North Kivu, which threatened regional stability, resulted in international attempts to settle the crisis. The governments of Rwanda and DRC took integrated measures to dissolve the FDLR in November 2007. One of the measures they agreed to take was the establishment of DRC government military operations against the FDLR. In addition, the two governments agreed to foster other armed groups in Eastern DRC.

A conference on security, peace and development was organized in Goma in January 2008 as a result of the failure of the government military against the CNDP. The FDLR wasn't invited to the conference, but the representatives of PARECO, Congolese armed groups, CNDP and Kivu civil society were present. The conference brought about the Act of Engagement, signed on 23 January 2008 by the representatives of each group. They started an instant cease-fire and the ongoing demobilization of their armed forces. Subsequently, the government decided to halt the threat made by the FDLR. It granted amnesty to Congolese armed forces who signed the Act of Engagement for acts of war, excluding war crimes or genocide and crimes against humanity. This process limited the amnesty to indulge in armed conflict but not to acts that involve severe human rights violations.

After the signing of the Act of Engagement, the cease-fire has been violated umpteenth times; many girls and women have been sexually abused, and children were recruited into the armed forces through scores of civilians' unlawful killings or abductions. Some people dwell as IDPs fear returning to their fields and homes. Foreign and Congolese armed forces are still controlling large parts of the district, and some of the FDLR persist to resist the repatriation and disarmament of Rwandan armed forces.

It's obvious that minerals are one of the powerful causes of the conflicts, but the primary connection between the waging war and North Kivu's resource wealth is complicated to decode. Le Billion observes that the main commodities are greatly amenable to looting and taxing and, thus, a means of prolonging and increasing conflict. Mineral resources aren't the main source of income for CNDP and M23 though they make huge money from it. The conflicts were about citizenship, land rights and demographics. The conflicts were not triggered by greed but by the belief that the DRC government couldn't safeguard the Tutsi population. Therefore, it's significant that attempts to comprehensively understand regional conflicts don't focus on economic issues but on social and political concerns.

Everything you need to know about the Kivu Conflict

In October 2022, the conflicts in the Eastern democratic republic of Congo elevated. The war between its army and M23 combatant group has caused civilians harm, demolished infrastructure, and cut off access to healthcare, food, and other necessary community needs.

There were gunshots in the North Kivu area, which led to mass displacement and massacre. The UN

Refugee Agency says, "Over 5.6 million populations were internally displaced while over 1 million sought refuge outside the country.

What fueled the conflict was a fight to control the DRC's abundant mineral resources, which are diamonds, oil, and gold and the biggest manufacturer of precious metals like gold, copper, cobalt, and tin. According to UN experts, Uganda and Rwanda's export of tin and gold came from the DRC as a means of exploitation.

M23 is one of the oppressive combat groups attacking the country. They constitute the great lakes region, considered a geopolitical battlefield comprising neighboring rivals such as Burundi, Uganda and Rwanda. The conflict precipitates from a severe history and a sudden call for peace; its destruction is still perpetuated with survivors caught in the crossfire.

What is the current situation?

Louise, a displaced mother at Kanyaruchinya IDP, says, "I had lost count of times I had to flee from the war when I was young, and now my children were born and bred in the same situation. I wished it wasn't the same with them."

The more the war heightens in the North Kivu province, the more dwellers are displaced. UNHCR Africa recorded over 5.8 million displaced populations in the North and South Kivu, Tanganyika and Ituri. More than 522,000 asylum-seekers and refugees in the DRC and 1 million DRC asylum-seekers and refugees outside DRC. In January 2023, over two hundred civilians were murdered in the Ituri area in various attacks by non-state rebel groups. The attack destroyed two thousand homes and demolished eighty schools.

The FARDC announced on 16 February 2023 that 356 Rwandan armed forces arrived in Congo. It's assumed that the M23 rebel group reinforces them.

The M23 rebel group consists of people who are not Congolese but are filtered into the country because of the Rwandese genocide. Hence, analyzing the facts and negotiation around the combatants' request to be incorporated into the DRC's security system is weird.

The renewal of the M23 combatants into the Eastern DRC emerged due to the agreement's failure to initiate the ex-army of Tutsis indigene into the Congolese defense system. Some of these terms are that the army from Rwanda Defense Force incorporated the DRC security forces, intelligence services, police and army. 99% of their force dwells in the east to safeguard Tutsis who are killed and prejudiced. Meanwhile, they're controlling the Eastern DRC with the remnant of the Uganda People's defense force and UPDF as their supporting system.

However, the wealth of DRC's resources triggers economic threats to its citizens and entitlement motivated by blood-lust, political leaders hiding behind combat groups to execute their sinister motives. Since the onset of the conflict, many corporations have hidden silently in the background, gaining from the bloodshed of innocents.

Key Takeaway

- Since December 1990, non-governmental organizations like Global Witness have been campaigning for auto-conflict minerals legislation and initiatives because revenue from these natural resources trigger conflicts. These campaigns established a UN Panel of Inquiry, passing a raft of legislation. Projects were established to reform the mining industry.

- The US Dodd-Frank Act was passed in July 2019. Afterwards, the DRC government banned mining in the Eastern provinces, leading to a de facto embargo on natural resources from North and South Kivu. Meanwhile, the suspension didn't bring the desired results. Armed forces appeared barely affected by the loss of revenue from natural resources, suddenly diversifying their revenue streams.

- The Kivu conflict has had a destructive impact on the DRC economy. Agricultural land was destroyed, and the dearth of land meant young ones could not become farmers.

- Large criminal operations perpetuate widely. Nevertheless, the belief that greed is prevalent in many theories of conflict and resources is incorrect. For those involved, the natural resources trade is the simplest way to survive in a community where poverty reigns.

Chapter 6: The Impacts of War on Our World

When it comes to war, no one is a victor because all the parties involved will suffer the consequences with large casualties. This chapter will explore the effects of war on politics, people, the environment, and the economy.

The Effects of War On People

The genuine victims of war can only be calculated based on the definition of victim. The definition may be based on the number of people who died due to violence or those who died from the epidemic, sexual violence or hunger during the war. It could also mean those who died after injuries or illnesses sustained in the war.

For instance, the consequence of the United States' intervention in Cambodia and Vietnam (1965-1975) offers a clear image of this issue. About three million people died in the Vietnam War.

Afterwards, the Vietnamese government claimed that over 42,000 people had died from accidents caused by old ammunition. During the conflict against the North Vietnamese forces, the United States armed groups used over 15 million tons of bombs and explosives, of which 80,000 tons polluted 20% of the country.

According to a German Nobel Prize winner for literature, Heinrich Böll, "As long as a wound inflicted is still somewhere bleeding, the war will never be over." He was describing the long-term impacts of wars. Whether soldiers or civilians, people affected by the war always nursed physical wounds for decades. Sometimes, the casualties of the war usually learn to live with mutilation after being deafened or blinded.

Another effect of war on victims is the psychological effect. The survivors will have to live in fear and insecurity daily. It might even be due to mental health disorders like anxiety, depression, and post-traumatic stress disorder (PSTD). These can happen to both soldiers and civilians.

The transformation of citizens into refugees is another effect of war on people. The United Nations recorded over 15 million refugees worldwide who left their homes because of wars or persecution. Three-quarters of them are living in developing nations.

The refugees and their children often suffer from malnutrition, hunger, diseases and ailments. The conflict has made them homeless and taken away their livelihoods. The condition of the refugees remains complicated when there's no long-term solution in view. Also, when they dwell in larger camps, various security threats may arise for them and their ecosystem, resulting in violent wars.

The Impact of War On Our Economy And Politics

One of the political impacts of a war is the truth that it can wipe out a community and state. Citizens' freedom is curtailed during the war. Freedom of speech, choice, a state of emergency, and other activities by societal or political groups are restricted during the war. The relationship between the two parties involved in the war will be broken and destroyed for many years. Even distrust will grow among the citizens with various opinions.

The 34th president of the US and supreme commander of the armed forces during the second world war, Dwight D. Eisenhower, lamented, "This world in wars is not spending funds alone but also spending the sweat of its workers, the hopes of its children and the genius of its scientists." According to Oxfam International, International Action Network on Small Arms and Saferworld, the following are among the costs of war:

- Increased military expenses that other industries of the economy lack.

- Destruction of infrastructure and livelihoods.

- Reduction of economic activities via insecurities, mobility and the allocation of civil labor to the armed forces and flight of capital.

- Macroeconomic impacts like limited saving, inflation, exports, investment and increased debt.

- Loss of development aid.

- Transfer of assets to the illegitimate economy.

The conquest of international territories and loss of the forced redistribution of land, means of labor and production.

The Impacts of War on Our Environment

The UN pronounced every November 6th as the INTERNATIONAL DAY FOR HEDGING AGAINST THE EXPLOITATION OF THE ENVIRONMENT IN WAR AND CONFLICTS in 2001. Kofi Annan, former UN General Secretary, wanted to create an awareness of the adverse ecological and environmental effects of conflicts that have destroyed humanity through direct violence. Destructions caused by chemicals, landmines, oil, or exploded military equipment usually take much time to repair; the pollution of air, water and soil threatens citizens' standard of living and causes them to flee.

Also, new technologies, like certain munitions and uranium, caused damage to the environment. The minute amounts of radioactive uranium can damage kidneys or other organs and cause cancer. Another effect of war on the environment is destroying natural resources for tactical reasons.

For instance, the bombardment of oil production facilities in the Gulf conflicts used to destroy the economy, the intentional mining of pastures to loot the enemy of its food supply or the usage of chemical warfare groups like Agent Orange used by the US in the Vietnam conflict as a defoliant to damage crop plants. The environment is also an innocent victim affected by the crossfire.

On the other hand, people experiencing poverty suffer mostly because they depend heavily on the environment for their livelihoods, such as food, medicine and tools for homes and shelter.

How Conflicts Shape Us

War is a force for transformation within societies and countries. The connection between war and society is cyclical because war impacts how places are named and people's language and fosters social changes. Despite its downsides, it compels people to contribute to society, especially in non-traditional ways. The positive societal transformations are voting rights and women's work following their contribution during the First and Second World Wars.

While evolution provided people with the potential to avenge violently, it also offered them the potential of altruism and killing others. In addition, if a nation celebrates battleground heroism frequently, the citizens love war.

Generally, communities can be trained to be warlike; meanwhile, they can transition to a peaceful community over time. Culture and group cohesion can majorly affect a society's will to combat. During the 19th century, the global democratic shift in governance enabled people to view themselves as citizens instead of subjects. The association belongs to a large stakeholder group that resulted in a heightened willingness to combat for one's nation; in a conflict such as World War I. Meanwhile, war is different from the range of acts of violence.

Rather, conflict is highly pre-planned and organized. Armies will be willing to kill and operate as part of an incorporated group because of the organized nature of the conflict. Some communities have made rules on how to conduct war ethically, including how to capture the army and treat civilians. Because of the country's ability to organize war and the connection between the community's view of war, information warfare would become highly significant for demoralizing enemies and rallying support in future wars.

An armed war may traumatize civilians and armies for the rest of their lives. The economic toll of the conflict is realistic and possible to aggregate measure. Meanwhile, it's impossible to discern the psychological effects of war. One of the overall health effects of wars on people is post-traumatic stress disorder, which is widely accepted and acknowledged. It has been treated with the help of psychedelic drug treatments and VR technology. But estimating the psychological cost of conflict may be impossible, although it is safe to utter that the cost is incredulously steep.

The Effects of War On Public Health

According to the WHO, over 1.8 billion people are presently living in war-affected places in the world. The public health effects of such is a reality.

War can result in a high mortality rate, the destruction of economic and social systems, hunger, several damages to health services, loss of medical supply chains, bad epidemic outbreaks and loss of healthcare practitioners. The emergence of bacteria has been associated with military operations, emitting new categories like pathologies of intervention. Psychological effects of conflict are deadly, with the prevalence of depression, post-traumatic stress disorder, somatoform disorder and anxiety disorder increasing in conflict and post-conflict settings. In 2017, about ten per cent of women and sixteen per cent of children were living dangerously close to conflict locations displaced by war. These made them susceptible to early marriage, isolation, exploitation, sexual violence, and harassment.

In addition, conflicts exclusively affect rural areas and have foreign repercussions. The war in Ukraine has led to adverse global effects on food and energy, inflation, repercussions of war beyond national borders and financial speculation.

It is not a mistake that the Charter of Ottawa mentions peace as the priority for health. Peace emits other determinants, such as education, income, decent housing, sustainable resources, a stable ecosystem, equity and social justice. Public healthcare practitioners have major roles to play when armed wars are considered, knowing the adverse effects of conflict, working to prevent conflict outbursts, and advocating for peace.

Key Takeaways

- Although no child has the right to encounter the horrors of conflict, many do. The impacts on children living with violent war are devastating and not often obvious. In 2018, over 357 million children were dwelling in war-affected locations.

- War doesn't only affect the access of children to education, and it also prevents their education from the early stage of life. Many children in Syria have experienced war for almost eleven years. Such children are counted as a lost generation when it comes to education. Research showed that war also adversely affects the physical and cognitive development of unborn babies whose mothers experienced war.

- The youngest children exposed to violent war can emit long-term adverse effects. The children have a healthy emotional mentality that they can trust their caregivers or parents to safeguard them from conflicts and meet their basic needs, which is the fundamental security attachment and growing liberation. But conflict instills in many children the fear that no one can safeguard them, whether through the death of their parents, physical wounds, or safe areas to play and sleep. This results in avoidance or risk-taking attitude and sleeplessness, depression and symptoms of post-traumatic stress disorder. This, in turn, affects children's potential to pursue their needs in the future, which can affect their mental health, developing a vicious cycle of marginalization. However, the impact of war on the disabled children is amplified. They are often abandoned and don't have access to fundamental needs.

- Though some pictures of war usually display young children as unintended victims, as collateral of armed wars, the truth is that those children are usually targets during the conflict, at threat of exploitation. During the war, the parents may be killed or wounded, and they cannot protect or provide for their little ones. In this context, children or their supporters can entertain threats they consider preferable to other dangers. This could be promising a younger girl to be married for money, compelling an early marriage on a young child or honoring the invitation of a third party who vows to meet the child's needs. Ultimately, the young child may become a laborer, trafficked, sent to combat as a combatant, or sexually exploited.

- Child army is always at risk of physical wound or death. They also experience emotional and sexual abuse. If they peradventure, they survive the war. They can be detained as perpetrators instead of victims, compounding the psychosocial effects of their exploitation. Child soldiers may tend to display more signs of mental health than children who suffer similar levels of trauma as non-combatants. In this type of exploitation, it is prevalent for a child to doubt their identity as victims, frequently resulting in self-blame and long-term tackling with unhealthy relationships with themselves and other people.

Epilogue

Throughout the chapters of this book, we have witnessed the profound impact of war on individuals, families, and nations. We have seen war's devastation and trauma, leaving lasting wounds that may never fully heal. We have heard the voices of those who have endured the horrors of armed conflict, pleading for peace, understanding, and a better future for generations.

As I reach the end of this journey through the pages of war, it is only fitting to reflect upon the profound cost and lasting impact of conflicts such as the Sierra Leone Civil War on our world. The tales of suffering and resilience, the scars etched upon the hearts and landscapes, are a stark reminder of the urgent need for peace and understanding. In this epilogue, I offer my reflections on the cost of war, the enduring hope for a better future, and our role in shaping it.

In all its grim realities, war exacts a heavy toll on humanity. It tears apart families, shatters communities, and leaves scars that can take generations to heal. The book's stories showcase people's immense struggles and incredible strength in overcoming them. However, it's not enough to simply observe and feel empathy. We must take action and use these stories to inspire positive change.

War creates violence, hatred, and revenge cycles, trapping future generations in despair. It affects society, leaving behind a legacy of trauma and division. It also takes resources away from endeavors such as education, healthcare, and infrastructure and directs them toward destructive actions. The impact of war surpasses the destruction and loss of life.

War exacts a heavy toll on individuals, families, and communities, tearing apart the very fabric of society. The harrowing tales of suffering and resilience showcased in this book expose the deep wounds inflicted by violence. These stories compel us to empathize and take concrete action to prevent such devastation from occurring again. We must harness the power of these narratives to inspire positive change in our communities, nations, and the world at large.

One of the most insidious legacies of war is perpetuating cycles of violence, hatred, and revenge. Unless we actively work to break these destructive patterns, future generations will continue to suffer the consequences. It is incumbent upon us to challenge the narratives of division and seek pathways to reconciliation and healing. By embracing the values of peace, dialogue, and understanding, we can create a ripple effect that extends far beyond our immediate surroundings.

We must also recognize that the impact of war extends far beyond the destruction and loss of life. It erodes the social fabric, exacerbates existing inequalities, and diverts valuable resources from important sectors such as education, healthcare, and infrastructure. By investing in peaceful resolutions and the reconstruction of war-torn societies, we can redirect these resources toward building sustainable and inclusive communities that prioritize the well-being of all their members.

In the face of darkness, there is always a glimmer of hope. The stories of resilience and the indomitable human spirit that emerged from the ashes of war offer us rays of light and inspire us to believe in the possibility of a better future. These stories remind us that healing, reconciliation, and renewal are attainable and essential for building a world that values peace, justice, and equality.

Each of us has a role in breaking the cycles of violence and building a world where conflicts are resolved through dialogue and understanding. It begins with acknowledging humanity in one another, embracing diversity, and fostering a culture of empathy and compassion. It requires us to confront our prejudices and biases, challenge the narratives of hatred and division, and actively work towards building bridges of peace. Although we cannot alter the past, we can influence and create a better future.

Education is a powerful tool in this endeavor. We must teach our children the futility of violence and the importance of empathy, nurturing a generation that seeks solutions through diplomacy and cooperation. Educating ourselves and future generations about the realities of war can sow the seeds of peace and create a world that values dialogue, justice, and equality.

The responsibility for peace and justice rests with individuals and those who hold power positions. We must also hold our leaders accountable. We must demand transparency, accountability, and ethical leadership from our governments and institutions. Only then can we ensure that the lessons of history are heeded and that the mistakes of the past are not repeated.

The path to peace may be challenging, requiring patience, perseverance, and unwavering commitment. It requires us to challenge the narratives that justify violence and embrace a vision of a world where conflicts are resolved through peaceful dialogue, justice prevails over vengeance, and compassion guides our actions.

Let us not forget that pursuing peace is not a passive endeavor but an active commitment that requires continuous effort. It necessitates a collective responsibility to address the root causes of conflicts, promote dialogue, and cultivate a culture of peace at every level of society. It begins with fostering understanding and empathy among individuals, extending to our families, communities, and the global stage.

We must foster a mindset that values diplomacy, negotiation, and compromise as the means to resolve disputes. This requires investing in diplomacy and conflict resolution mechanisms, strengthening international institutions, and promoting multilateral cooperation. By prioritizing peaceful solutions, we can prevent conflicts from escalating into full-scale wars and spare countless lives from suffering and devastation.

Furthermore, we must address the underlying issues contributing to the outbreak of conflicts, such as social injustice, economic disparities, and political instability. By addressing these root causes, we can create a more equitable and inclusive world where people have access to opportunities, their voices are heard, and grievances can be addressed peacefully.

At the same time, we must strive to build bridges of understanding and reconciliation between communities torn apart by conflicts. Healing war wounds requires fostering dialogue, promoting forgiveness, and supporting rebuilding trust among individuals and communities. Through these efforts, we can lay the foundation for sustainable peace and prevent future generations from inheriting a legacy of violence.

The power to shape a peaceful future lies within every one of us. We can challenge the status quo, advocate for change, and be catalysts for peace in our spheres of influence. We can engage in constructive dialogue, promote tolerance and respect, and reject the temptation to resort to violence or hatred in the face of disagreements.

Let us not underestimate the impact of our actions. Each act of kindness, each effort to build bridges, and each commitment to nonviolence contribute to a ripple effect that extends far beyond what we can imagine. By inspiring others through our words and actions, we can create a groundswell of support for peace and set a chain of events in motion that lead to a more harmonious and just world.

In conclusion, I implore you to carry the stories you have encountered within these pages into your hearts. These should serve as a reminder of the toll of war on humanity and the pressing need for peace. Embrace the power within you to effect change, no matter how small it may seem.

The journey through this book may end here, but the pursuit of peace continues. May we all play our part in building a world where the tales of war are confined to the pages of history and where the voices of peace and reconciliation echo loudly for generations to come.